A Rollercoaster of Emotions

Keisha Fredericks

BookLeaf Publishing

India | USA | UK

Presentation by *BookLeaf Publishing*

Web: www.bookleafpub.com

E-mail: info@bookleafpub.com

ISBN: 9789358318760

First edition 2023

To my mother—Pauline Fredericks—whose voice still guides me.

1952 - 2021

A new day

Everyday I wake I expect something new
A glimmer of hope I will make it through

Today's a new day yesterday's the past
Learning to let go and live in the present
sometimes it's hard

But what choice do I have
Unless I want to not move
I learnt from a young age
That it's all down to you

No feeling is permanent this I know is true

So even on my worse days I know better days
are due

Celebrate

First and foremost I celebrate my life
I celebrate me and my drive to fight
I celebrate all the trials that I've won
I celebrate the lessons I've learnt the good and
the bad
I celebrate my mum and I celebrate my dad
I celebrate the present cause the past can not be
changed
I celebrate the future cause it's a brand new day
I celebrate that I'm able to do what I want and
more
I celebrate my smile cause it wasn't always there
I celebrate the ones around me that really care
I celebrate the haters you've made your motive
clear
I celebrate me cause I always hold it down
I celebrate reality ten toes on the ground

Freedom

No shackles on my feet but I don't feel free

Plugged into a system in order to eat

At birth we're registered

At death it's the same

Today I woke up at 6:30am to be at work at 8

It could all be so simple but the prices inflate

I love when I take a holiday out of the U.K.

It reminds me of freedom as I stay on the beach
the whole day

To live doesn't mean you're alive, no cliche

Most people look at freedom as being financially
free

Some people need the freedom around the
world—refugees

So much politics and war sometimes there's no
chance to be free

I can count myself lucky that I grew where I did

In a lot of countries people don't get to be kids

How can I really be free if most of the world is
not

Freedom to me is when the whole world is free

A better day for you and better day for me!

The state of the world

The state of the world right now is absolutely in
bits

There's too much to ignore and to try would be a
sin

It could all be so simple but the politics cause
rifts

There's enough land in the world for everyone to
live

To grow food and raise kids without having to
worry

I get so angry when I see the news

So many one sided stories nations abused

Why can't people just let people live

War crimes everywhere but many will be
ignored

So much injustice it's the same old tale I'm
bored

Sometimes change will take long cause it's fixed
from inside

But I'm a believer in everything has it's time

Everything has its course like the end of the line

Right and wrong everything's in our face

Blatant genocide whole countries erased

In ten years time the history books will be a
disgrace.

So help who you can and when the time's right
you'll know

And as I end this poem lord have mercy on our
souls

My Mother

Born in Kingston Jamaica in 1952

That generation I can't even imaigne what you
went through

You were apart of the windrush era when you
first came to the U.K. soil

A proud woman ready for it all

I learnt from the best whether right or wrong

And because of you I have wisdom that will live
on

You were truly one of a kind

You left a big legacy behind

And I am Keisha Fredericks I carry your light

Things between us weren't always good

But you had my back if the shove came to push

We only get one mother and I understand that
more now

The first person we turn to no matter how old we
get

An award a milestone or any bit of good or bad
news

Now I just look to the sky cause my heart feels
blue

To have one more conversation with you I wish I
could do

I miss my Mum I never imagined life without
you

Friends

My mother always told me that you can count
your true friends on one hand

When I was younger I never thought that to be
true

Thought everyone had my back it was such a big
crew

But the older I got the more I saw

That some of them were never my friends at all

Actions speak louder than words and that's a
fact

And not physically but I've been stabbed in the
back

Took me a while to see but it's oh so clear

That the length of time you know someone
means nothing I swear

I can't call everyone a friend cause that word
carries weight

Through mental health and bereavement you'll
see who's fake

I've met some real ones in the past few years

Just one or two let me make that clear

One good friend that's all you really need

And if you've found or got that one you'll
understand what I mean

One real friend can feel like a whole team

So shout out to the real ones cause you've
become family

OCD

OCD will make me never give up

Got to get it all perfect let's do it again

I used to like the number 2 now I like the
number 4

And if I don't repeat an action 4 times,
OCD will make me do it even more

The volume on the tv has to be right

Cause if it's on the wrong number OCD will bite

Growing up I didn't really understand what it
was

Doing weird rituals would make it all stop

But just for a minute cause OCD is deep in the
mind

I think stress triggers it more and the
compulsions get worse

Uncontrollable and recurring thoughts

Fear of contamination or dirt to me this is the
worst

I can't even eat from a plate in my cupboard
without washing it 4 times first

OCD is chronic and there is no cure

You can get it under control but it's always there

I would love to wake up one day with my
thoughts clear

Death

If there's one thing in life that's certain it's death

No one can escape it or know where and when

Tomorrow's not promised no matter who you are

You could try to cross the road and get hit by a
car

Life and death go hand in hand

It's the circle of life the creator's plan

I sometimes wonder what happens when we die

And will I see my mum again,
Has she been waiting in the sky?

There has to be more to it that we're yet to
understand

Cause the sudden death of a loved one doesn't
feel like a plan

We got one life to live so it's best to try and do it
right

Cause when you're gone that's it so make sure
your legacy's prime

Life

Life can only get better can't stay forever cold

Cause after the rain the sunshine's on the road

And after the night a new morning unfolds

You've got to keep strong to see what the day holds

Travel

Travel to me is a way a to see,
Different lifestyles and scenery

Something that you can not find at home,
A beautiful view that will fill your soul

To clear your mind and to have a think ,
To take some time out when you've reached the
brink

Therapy without meds I'll take that any day
Put me on a warm sandy beach let me watch the
waves

I'm not sure what it is but I feel good when I
travel
The experiences and memories implanted in my
brain

Learning from the different cultures and
similarities in human race

I cherish it all today's a better day

Mental health

It's important to focus on your mental health
cause feeling right inside is truly wealth

Sometimes you have to just put yourself first, set
boundaries and know your worth

The world often feels like it goes way too fast
With not enough time to process it's hard

What works for them may not work for you
Got to find your balance got to make it through

Depression is real and the numbness can kill
Low mood all around that lasts for months or
weeks

Coping with the stresses of life,
1 in 4 people would have been affected by a
mental illness at sometime

Makes up for 14.3% of deaths worldwide
That's why it's nice to be nice and good to be
kind

Happiness

Happiness to me is made up of so many things

Happiness is when the food tastes right and it hits the spot

Happiness is getting paid and it's all paid off

Happiness is a new season of your favourite show

Happiness is when you order an outfit and the size fits right

Happiness is waking up and seeing a new day

Happiness is seeing my nephew and his happy little face

Happiness is the weekend no work today

Happiness is the weather staying sunny and bright

Happiness is getting into your bed at night

Happiness is hearing and vibing to your
favourite song

Happiness is being surrounded by the ones you
love

Happiness comes in many forms
And it can be found in many things
Your happiness is down to you it's your song to
sing

I love

I love warm summer nights
I love a cold morning breeze
I love the sound of the rain
I love the raindrops when they freeze

I love the sound of the birds
I love the blossoms on a tree
I love the flowers when they bloom
I love watching the sprout of a seed

I love being on a boat at sea
I love looking at the clouds out the plane
I love being on long road trips
I love the cross country trains

I love hearing my music loud
I love when I discover new songs
I love music as a love language
I love when the bass hits and it's strong

I love home cooked food
I love spice in my meals
I love the smell of a bbq
I love trying different foods

I love my own space
I love taking time out to think
I love when it all comes together
I love when it all makes sense

Alcohol

I've been drinking more in the last two years
than I have in my whole life

A shot for breakfast made the morning bright

It's not normal but it helped me to cope

Waking up with headaches you would've
thought I've learnt

But the addiction to alcohol was too much it
hurt

Any excuses for a drink I'd find one any day

Work just finished now pour me all the way

One of the worst demons that I faced in my life

To kick the habit everyday I tried

No drink today to myself I would say

Then order some bottles and give into the crave

It got like this when I lost my mum

To numb it all out I would drink to get drunk

The day I really stopped was the day I knew

That it was time for change the sobriety was
overdue

Character

My mum was very old fashioned

When I was younger I told her I was depressed and she said me too

She came from the era where depression was a taboo

Where you get up and work and just push through

I used to think that was the way to be

Now I know that's wrong

But I'm thankful cause it made me strong

Character building can come in many forms

And the lessons I've learnt have made me who I am

Through the good and the bad solid as a rock I stand

Imagine

Mountain tops and the tops of trees

Skyscrapers up thousands of feet

The seven wonders of the world
Unknown wonders of the sea

All the stars in the sky
Big enough for us to see

All the colours in the flowers
Sweet honey from a bee

Sunrise in the morning
Sunset in the eve

Work

There has to be a balance between work and
home
Cause some of these companies will drain your
soul

Living each day on autopilot strapped to a seat
It gets repetitive like Monday the start of another
week

Work the hours monthly then repeat
Looks good from the outside like life's sweet

Ever stayed in a job for longer than you need
Money may be good but are you coping
mentally

Working from home has been a blessing in
disguise
It proves that it's possible and the companies
survived

The stress it takes out of going into the job
And the time it takes to travel to and from can be
long

There has to be a balance between work and
home
Cause some of these companies will drain your
soul

I wanna

I wanna see the world there's a lot I wanna do

I wanna hike the canyons and take in the views

I wanna see the pyramids and get lost in the
mystery and really feel the meaning of history

I wanna climb Mount Everest and feels the chills

I wanna live my life with the freedom of day no
9 to 5 stress for the minimum wage

I wanna party all night and sleep all day,
Cause sometimes life's a party we need to
celebrate

I wanna quit my job in the funniest of ways and
tell my boss where to stick his pay

I wanna wake up each day with no stress on my
mind

I wanna live my life before it's the end of my
time

War

War is not the answer it never has been

It just leads to destruction and all types of sin

The natural balance of the world is no longer a thing

Land's controlled by man, what makes it theirs?

Families displaced and nobody cares

Throughout history there has always been wars

They've got money to fight but can't feed the poor

How can we be ok with living in a world like this

Where positions of power get misused it's so sad

A million for a war head instead of helping who needs

Something so simple like a water supply and
tools to thrive

But instead a one time bomb is dropped from the
sky

Destruction all around and bloodied children cry

History will never be pretty and most of it will
be lies

Motions

I didn't wanna get out of bed today so I stayed in
bed for most of the day
Another day wasted but what can I say

These battles I fight on the surface you can't tell
Cause I hold my own and carry myself well

It's hard to be motivated sometimes and it's hard
being optimistic too
But on my darkest days I know there's a way
through

You could call it depression, you could call it
grief, you could call it being lazy, but taking
time out sometimes is what we all need

I try to stay positive in all that I do
I'd rather see you smile than feel my blues
Cause misery loves company so solo I move

Tomorrow will be a better day that's what I tell
myself when I'm feeling down

I'm just going through the motions but there's a
calm in the storm now

She

She found beauty in the world
but the world messed her over,

Peace in her soul when she decided to be sober

She felt presence in the world when she looked a
little deeper

Love in her heart even though it grew colder.....